Wreath For The Earth?

Wreath For The Earth?

Elegy for the Ecology
Eulogy for the Encroaching Pollution

PART -1 OF POEMS TO PERUSE, PONDER, PURSUE
(Free-Translation of own poems from Hindi)

VERSES FOR THE ELDERLY & GROWN-UPS

Subhash S. Naik

PARTRIDGE

To order additional copies of this book, contact
Partridge India
000 800 10062 62
orders.india@partridgepublishing.com

www.partridgepublishing.com/india

Contents

Elegy - 2

Elegy - 3

Elegy - 4

Resurrection

Poet:
Subhash S. Naik
Flat-1, Jay Krupa, TPS-6,
Opposite Sambhaji garden,
Near Milan-Subway,
Santacruz(West),
Mumbai (Bombay) -400054.
INDIA.
M: 91-9869002126.
eMail: vistainfin@yahoo.co.in
Website: www.subhashsnaik@com

Cover Design:
Girija Kannal Bhadadia.
Eeksha Design & Communication
Vadodara (Baroda), Gujarat, INDIA.
M- 91-9737299749.
eMail:eeksha.design@gmail.com

Dedication

Dedicated to Mr. Al Gore, (Former Vice-President of USA), for his untiring efforts towards spreading the message of the dangers of damaging the Environment, and his message of environment-protection for a better future of mankind.

Introduction

Nearly 6 years ago, my first book of English poems on Environment & Pollution, titled 'The Earth In Custody' was published. It was sponsored by D.L. Shah Trust, Mumbai.

I have been a member of the Solar Energy Society of India, and have been interested in Alternate Energy. Also, a number of years ago, I had read the book 'Limits to Growth', which is a Report prepared by a multidisciplinary group of scientists called 'Club of Rome'. It highlighted that the natural resources in the world will run out in a few years' time, if the human race does not do anything about it. In spite all this, I wonder whether I would have written any poems on Pollution & Environment, had the D.L. Shah Trust not decided to produce a Hindi TV Serial for children, on Environment & Pollution. That inspired me to write on this subject, and I was fortunate that 6-7 of my Hindi poems were used in the Serial. Later I also wrote some poems on this subject in English. Shortly thereafter, the same Trust sponsored the Development of a Training Program for School-Teachers, on Environment & Pollution. It was developed by TERI (The Energy & Research Institute), a highly reputed organization in this field. Here too, I was fortunate that 2-3 poems of mine were used in the Training Program.

Soon after my abovementioned book of English poems was published, I felt that I should translate my Hindi poems in English, so that they could be read by people who are not familiar with Hindi. One of those collections is the present Book, 'Wreath for The Earth?'. Another similar book of poems translated into English, and titled 'Heal The Bleeding Earth', is also expected to published shortly after the publication of the present book. Three books of Hindi poems on the same subject (books from which I have selected the poems for translation) are also on the way to publication.

I have not written these poems to get name & fame (which anyway does not matter at my stage of life); but merely because I felt that an expression on this important subject should reach the people. A number of Technical articles on this subject appear in the media, and a number of reports on international conferences held. But mine is different way, a creative way, to approach this very important subject.

For the Foreword to this book, I had approached two eminent persons, personally known to me, one in India & the other in USA. Both appreciated the importance of this venture & promised to write the foreword. However, VIPs have a number of commitments, and somehow the efforts to get the Forewords from them did not fructify. As you will see in a further paragraph, I too was quite tied up and could not maintain a sustained follow up for this purpose.

This book should have come out 2 years ago, and the representatives of the publishers, M/s Partridge, have been following up with me ceaselessly. However, they understood my difficulties and waited patiently. For that I must thank them.

I would also like to show my appreciation to the cover-designer, Ms. Girija Kannal-Bhadadia, who has designed an excellent and most appropriate cover, and waited with great understanding for publication of the book.

The delay was caused by the illness due to cancer, of my dear wife Dr. Snehalata, a social-scientist. Unfortunately, she succumbed to the disease a few months back. Although this is a profound loss, very difficult for me to bear, I felt that the work on an important subject like Pollution & Environment, should reach the people. So I have temporarily kept personal grief aside, and have proceeded to finalize the manuscript for publication.

Although I am holding Engineering & management qualifications, and though I have worked as a Senior Corporate Executive in my professional career, I have always been interested in writing & literature, and, as time permitted, I continued to write poems & articles in English, Hindi/Hindustani & in my mother-tongue, Marathi. Some of this matter has been published in reputed publications over the years. But I feel that the present venture of poetry-books on Environment & Pollution could be the most relevant of my published & yet-unpublished works, for the society at large.

I do hope that those who would read this book would like it. But more importantly, I feel that even if a few of them are inspired to act towards Environment-protection, I would feel that the purpose of this book has been met.

+ + +

Subhash S. Naik
Mumbai, India.
11th May, 2016.

The Don

Pollution the Don is waiting with a wreath
Is it for the Nature? Is it for the Earth?
Don't just stand impassively, for you may find
That, this wreath is for the Mankind!

- - -

Elegy - 1

Description

'Whom do these characteristics describe? -
Omnipresent ....
Present everywhere, in every nook and corner
Omniscient ....
All-encompassing vision, spanning the whole world
Omnipotent ....
Strong beyond imagination, invincible.'

'I am sure, you are describing ...
All-powerful
Pollution'.

- - -

Definition

What is -
Creation ....**Of the People**
Empowered .... **By the People**
Unavoidable .... **For the People**?

Democracy? .....
Possibly.
Pollution? ....
Definitely!

- - -

Characteristics

Liberty, Independence;
Freedom;
Equality;
Opportunity;
These are the characteristics of Democracy.

But, it is equally true that,
Everyone is Independent; and
Nobody can order anyone
To reduce Pollution.

Everybody is Free
To act as he likes.
One can generate as much Pollution as one wants.

continue..

Everybody is equal.
Big or small, all can
Equally generate Pollution,
Equally scatter garbage around,
Equally dump unclean, unhygienic items.

Compare:
This is Democracy, and
This is Pollution.
Let's see, whether
The weight of democracy
Tilts the scale towards
Increasing Pollution, or decreasing it.

- - -

Oath

This is my country
I am its citizen.
And –
I have full right to
Pollute it.

- - -

Tug Of War

There is an ongoing
Tug of War
Between
the civilization and Pollution.
No one knows
Who will win.

But before deciding
on that Tug of War;
it is essential that,
the other Tug of War,
that between
developed and developing nations,
should first come to an end.

- - -

Kite

Progress is a kite,
which is being flown
by the Nature,
and the Human being is the 'maanza'
the agent strengthening the thread
connecting the flyer and the kite.

The Human feels that
it is he who is flying the kite.
He does not know, that
the thread called the civilization
can break any moment.

- - -

Ostrich

The ostrich
sits with its head buried in sand.
It thinks that,
this way,
the storm will pass on
without touching it,
and it will remain secure.

A cyclone
called Pollution & Global warming
is roaring, and
the Nature & Human civilization
are in danger.

continue..

But,
even now,
this flock of six billion ostriches
is impervious of this hazard,
thinking that,
the storm will pass on
without touching it.

But,
this cyclone
will not pass on;
it is here to stay.

- - -

Help-Line

The Government commissioned
A Help-Line
which can be used
in emergencies.

One day,
the receptionist at the Help-Line
received a call –
'Please help me!
There is an emergency.
I am the Nature.
Dastardly Human race
Has gravely injured me.
I might die any time!
Help! Help!'

continue..

Now,
where should the poor receptionist
pass on this information,
And, to whom?
In Mumbai?
In Delhi?
Or, in the United Nations?

The receptionist was baffled,
and kept on thinking.
The Nature
kept on shrieking, imploring, begging.

The receptionist kept the phone down.
The Nature's cries for help
were cut-off half-way.

- - -

VRS

The Nature
Dedicatedly served the Human being;
Gave all that was possible,
More than possible.

And,
the Human
took full advantage of it,
undue advantage.

Finally,
the disease called Pollution
pounced on the Nature,
it endangered the nature's life.

The Nature
was then sick and tired of everything,
and told the Human –
'I am resigning from your service,
I am taking VRS.
Now face the music!
Feel the wrath of life!'

- - -

VRS: Voluntary Retirement from Service.

SMS

I get repeated messages
on my mobile phone -
'If you see something
that has been left by an unknown person,
and if you suspect that it is dangerous,
please inform the police.'

Everyday I see polluting heaps of garbage
that are left there by unknown persons,
no one would claim their ownership.
I know that they are dangerous.
And I suspect that
they will destroy the civilization.

But, the police are helpless.
Now, whom should I get in touch with?

- - -

SMS - Short Messaging Service.
These are messages received on,
or sent from, mobile phones.

Mayhem

There's mayhem everywhere.
Schools of fishes
are fluttering and dying;
Flocks of birds
are falling down,
flopping their wings uselessly;
Herds of animals
are scurrying here and there,
making vain attempts to save own life.
The enemy's mighty army
has made a concerted merciless attack,
and has brought about
destruction and death everywhere.
No one can survive this havoc,
this killing spree,
of this foe,
the emperor,
the devil incarnate
named Homo Sapiens.

- - -

The Trickster

One is a playboy,
the other, a trickster.

The playboy
relishes all worldly pleasures.
He cares only for his own gratification.
He has
palaces, vehicles, money.
He has all the tools at his service,
for satisfying his desires.
The playboy just wants his enjoyment;
He does not bother about
its ill-effects.

continue..

The Trickster is very clever,
who keeps changing his forms,
who creates illusions
in order to achieve the objective.
The trickster
cares for the result of
own provocative action,
because the trickster wants to win;
and,
victory will definitely be the Trickster's.

Yes, the Playboy, Homo Sapiens
Will be annihilated by
The Trickster, Pollution.

- - -

Poison

Lord Shiva drank Halaahal,
the Deadly Poison.
Saint Meera accepted and drank
a cup of Poison.
Philosopher Socrates
willingly chose to drink
Hemlock, the poison,
with his own hands,
and die.

We are not Lord Shiva.
Nor are we Socrates,
Nor are we Meera, nor saints.
And, still,
We have to face a poisonous world.

continue..

Every moment,
we keep drinking
this Halaahal called Pollution.
Even though our innards burn,
we have to go on living.

Will we die like Socrates?
Will the Human race
die through its own deeds?
Before that happens,
we must destroy
this poison
Called Pollution.

- - -

Yajna

The Yajna is in progress.
The Emperor is performing the Yajna.
The Ritvij is officiating at the Yajna.
Smoke is rising high from the Yajna-Kunda,
Flames too rise.
Poor goat is being sacrificed
in the Yajna.
A great achievement!

Another yajna is in progress.
Emperor Pollution is performing the yajna.
The Human is the Ritwij,
officiating at this yajna.
The whole Earth is the yajna-kunda,
from which
polluted fumes are rising
and the flame of destruction.
And, in this yajna,
poor nature is being sacrificed.
A great achievement?

- - -

continue..

Yajna: Ancient Indian sacrifice-ritual,
performed at the fire.
Ritwij: A priest who officiates at the yajna.
Yajna-Kunda: The site, the pit,
where the yajna-fire is lit.

The End Of Existence

1. If anyboby wants to end his existence,
    No need to commit suicide,
    No need for Prayopaveshan,
    No need for Santhara,
    No need for seppuku.
    It is sufficient
    to breathe the poison named air,
    and drink the poisonous water
    trickling down from the taps
    in any metropolis.
    That's all.

-

continue..

2. Why do you struggle
   to get a law enacted
   for the right to
   oneself's own decision to die.
   Everybody already has that right!
   Just drink a few drops of water
   Contaminated by this twenty-first century.
   That's enough.
   Your purpose will be served.

   - - -

Prayopaveshan, Santhara, Seppuku:
Methods for ending one's own life with dignity.

Tape-Recorder

The tape-recorder in the car
Was playing a song –
'O traveller, wake up'.
It was adding –
'He who keeps sleeping,
loses everything'.
It was taunting –
'O Sinners,
when will you rid yourselves of sins?'
It was warning –
'No use repenting
after the crop is destroyed
by preying-birds'.

The tape was rewound automatically,
and the song was being played repeatedly-
'O traveller, wake up;
Wake up, O traveller'.

continue..

But the driver was the Homo Sapiens.
He was asleep while driving;
A deep sleep, unmindful of the happenings.

The Homo Sapiens kept on sleeping.
In the sleep,
his foot kept on pressing the accelerator.
The speed of the car increased,
And increased further,
And kept on increasing.
As it was, the fog called Pollution
Made it difficult to see;
And on top of that,
a napping driver,
and the speeding vehicle.

. . .

continue..

Finally,
The inevitable happened –
The car named Civilization
met with a serious accident.
It fell down a ravine,
And got battered badly.
The Driver, the Homo sapiens,
got gravely injured.

And still,
the tape-recorder
kept on repeating –
'O traveller, wake up;
Wake up, O traveller'.

- - -

Audit

Every few decades,
God audits
The Earth's Books of Accounts.

Recently, He conducted an Audit.
"What's this?", God exclaimed,
"Your accounts do not balance;
The Credits and Debits,
Income and Expenditure
do not balance out.
Such a thing
Never happened in the past".

The Earth
tried to render an explanation –
"There is a problem
with only one Account,
all the rest are OK".
"Which Account?", God enquired.
"The Account belonging to Homo Sapiens",
the Earth replied,
"he does not deposit anything useful,
just goes on withdrawing.
Because of him,
the health all other Accounts too
is endangered".

continue..

God warned the Earth,
"This way,
you will be bankrupt in no time".
"But, what to do?",
the forlorn Earth said desperately,
"This callous Homo Sapiens
just doesn't bother!"
"Do one thing", God advised,
"Immediately
write-off and close
the Homo Sapiens' Account".

- - -

Terrorists

My territory
has been infiltrated
by Terrorists.
They are
Destroying happiness,
Spreading violence,
Rendering deaths.

They are
bursting destructive bombs,
which are spreading poisonous gases;
They are
killing millions
and maiming billions.

There's devastation everywhere,
Peace is non-existent;
This garden of Eden is breaking up.

continue..

These extremists are suicide-killers,
unafraid of ending their own existence
for the sake of annihilation of Peace.

I have been crying out,
crying out for long –
'Somebody wake up
and save me
from these
polluting, destructive extremists,
called Human Beings.'

I, the injured helpless Earth,
Have been screaming and imploring;
But Alas!
The terror struck by
These extremists, this Human Race,
is going on increasing,
Ever-increasing!
Alas!!

- - -

<u>Elegy - 2</u>

The Dacoit

This is not the ancient tale
of the dacoit Ratnakar,
who became Valmiki the Sage;
This is the story of another dacoit,
a neo-Ratnakar, named
Homo Sapiens.

This dacoit
used to loot all those around him.
One day, he captured
an old couple, named
'Nature' and 'Earth'.
The dacoit threatened,
"I will take way
all that belongs to you,
and thereafter,
I will take your lives too."
The first aged one said,
"We are old, and have lived long.
We are not afraid of losing our lives."
The other said,
"But, tell us one thing –

continue..

You have been looting all and sundry
for such a long time,
you must have amassed abundant wealth.
Why don't you stop this despised work
of looting others?"

"It's for the sake of my children",
replied the dacoit,
"I carry on this looting
in order that
my children would get lots of wealth
and a happy life free from worries."

On hearing this,
First of the two old ones said,
"Do you know that
it was we who had donated the wealth
and helped all those travellers
whom you later looted? . . .

Now, if you will kill us,
from where will the other travellers
get their wealth?
And then, from where will you get yours,
For passing on to your children?"

continue..

The Second one
Continued the dialogue,
"Tell me,
Have you informed your children
about your heinous deeds?
Have you enquired what **they** desire?
After all,
all your deeds are for their sake.
Should you not ask them their opinion?
Do one thing,
Go and ask your children.
We will stay put here."

The dacoit
Went and talked to his children.
He told them what he had been doing;
He asked them what their opinion was
and what their wishes were.
The children replied,
"Did we tell you loot others
in order to amass wealth for us?
Did we tell you
to terminate the old couple, Nature and Earth?
And,
If taking the lives of Nature and Earth
is going to harm our interest,

continue..

is it not foolish to slay them?
Are you doing us a favour
Or are you spoiling our future?
Is it your wish that
we should curse you on growing up?"

This reply
was totally unexpected.
The Dacoit was taken aback.
He was perplexed;
He just couldn't decide
what to do next.   . . . . .
He is still wondering.
He is still unable to act,
not knowing what to do.

*

continue..

Oh yes,
In the ages past,
there was a dacoit Ratnakar,
who was transformed
on hearing
the frank eye-opening words
of his children.
He became Valmiki the Sage,
the creator of the Epic, Ramayana.

What will happen to
This other Dacoit
This neo-Ratnakar,
named Homo Sapiens?
Will he be transformed?

No one knows;
Even the God doesn't.

- - -

Shravan

"We desire
a pilgrimage to Varanasi",
Shravan's parents told him.
"That's simple", said Shravan,
"I will take you in our air-conditioned car".
So all three started for Varanasi
in their car.

On the way,
Shavan's parents felt thirsty.
Shravan's mother told him,
"Son, we are thirsty,
and our stock of mineral water
is also exhausted".
"Mother, I too am thirsty.
But the next town is quite far away.
If we come across a 'dhhabaa',
we will surely get mineral water there".
The car kept on moving ahead,
But they did not see any 'dhhabaa'.
Their thirst kept on increasing.

continue..

After some distance,
They saw a spring flowing nearby.
"Let's drink a little water here.
It is bound to be cool and pure";
said Shravan.

Shravan went to the spring
and filled up an empty bottle.
'Let me take a sip here itself",
he thought.
As soon as he drank a few drops of water,
He fell down, dead.
The 'arrow' named contaminated-water,
that was shot by
the neo-Dashrath named Pollution
had killed Shravan instantly.

. . . .

Shavan died,
But the hunter,
the neo-Dashrath named Pollution,
did not shed tears of repentance.
This neo-Dashrath waited
for the arrival of
another Shravan,
another new victim.

- - -

New Panchtantra

After a long time,
Panchtantra's Damanaka and Karataka
met again.
Damanaka told a story to Karataka.

"This is an ancient tale.
There was a mother,
a mother named Earth.
The mother had many children,
and she did everything possible
for bringing up the children.
Every one received all that was desired.
All the children lived together happily –
Eagles, sparrows, lions, cows, goats & sheep,
insects & fishes, trees & creepers,
all living beings, all living things.

"Amongst the children, there was one,
named Homo Sapiens.
He was selfish, greedy, crooked.
He wanted the entire wealth for himself.
And, he started taking it.
Mother Earth did not object.

continue..

Homo Sapiens
shamelessly started looting, plundering.
"Mother Earth tried to reason with him.
'Son', she said, 'Your plunder has wounded me,
and if you continue with this,
my very life will be endangered.'
Homo Sapiens callously replied,
'I have to fulfill my needs.'
On hearing this,
angry Mother Earth cursed Homo Sapiens thus –
'As you would damage my health more & more,
you will find breathing more and more difficult.
If you try to finish me off,
that will bring about your own end too'!"

. . . .

On completing the story, Damanaka asked,
"O Karataka, tell me,
What is the moral of this story?"
Karataka replied,
"I know Homo sapiens.
I have understood the moral of the story very well,
and it is this –
If, like Homo sapiens,
anyone endangers the life of one's own mother,
then, that will be one's own end too."

continue..

"Absolutely right", said Damanaka,
"Times have changed,
the Era has changed,
but, the moral of the story
has remained unchanged;
Because,
the behavior of Homo Sapiens too
has remained unchanged.

- - -

Kalp-Vriksha

This old tale
is about Kalp-Vriksha,
the Wish-fulfilling Tree.

One traveller,
very tired from his journey,
saw a tree
and rested in its shed.
It was Kalp-Vriksha;
But the traveler did not know that.

The traveler thought,
'I have traveled so long in hot Sun,
how nice it would be to get
a glass of cold water
to quench my thirst'.
Lo!
A glass of ice-cold water
appeared near him.

continue..

After drinking the water,
the traveler said,
'I am so hungry;
how I wish
I could get something to eat'.
And, instantly
a plate full of delicacies
appeared in front of him.

Now, the traveller's imagination ran wild,
and he desired,
'Wouldn't it be just great
if a beautiful woman with a fan
attends to me while I am eating?'.
Behold!
Instantly, a gorgeous woman
appeared next to the traveller.

. . . .

Till now,
the traveller had not given much thought
to the occurrences.
But, he was startled on seeing
the beauty appear so suddenly.
'My God!
From where has this damsel turned up?
Is this a Ghost?'

continue..

As soon as
this thought sprung in the traveller's mind,
the beauty
turned into a hedious ghost.
The traveler was terrified.
"Ghost! Ghost!", he shouted,
"Will it eat me?"
And,
Just as he uttered these words,
the ghost gobbled him up!

*

This nature
is just like Kalp-Vriksha.
Whatever the Human imagines,
The Nature
gives him all that,
in fact, much more.
Now,
The Human has started thinking
About a Ghost.
And,
Lo!
The horrible Pollution-Ghost
has made its appearance.

continue..
⦿⁓

The Human is afraid –
'Will this ghost finish me off?'
Behold!
The Pollution-Ghost
Has started ending the Human's existence!

*

Will the story
of Kalp-Vriksha
have the same ending
every time?

- - -

The Avatars Of Pollution

O Human,
No more will you see
Lord Vishnu's incarnation.
Revere these Avatars of Pollution.

Matsya: The Fish:
The water-borne pollution
arose through water
and spread everywhere.
Koorma: The Turtle:
Pollution came crawling slowly,
and reached us
before anybody realized.
Varaha: The Boar:
Pollution came charging
and rammed,
before Human Race could save itself.
Narsimha: The Half-Human Half-Lion Being:

continue..

Just like Narsimha,
who tore up Hiranyakashyap,
Pollution has torn up
the core of the world's peace.
Vaaman: The small, unimpressive one:
At first,
Pollution looked small, insignificant.
But, just like Vaaman,
without any effort on its part,
it occupied the whole earth.

But, these are only five.
There are supposed to be Ten Avatars.
What about the remaining five?

Why do you need five more?
They will be wasted.
Now, Pollution has covered the whole world,
It has pushed down the mighty Human,
dethroned him.
Yes, five Avatars of Pollution are enough.

. . . .

continue..

Still, if you wish,
Hear about the Tenth Incarnation.
Hear about –
Kalki: The Incarnation of the future.
On Kalki's arrival,
The World will come to an end.

O My! O My!
Kalki is already here
In form of Pollution.
Is this then
The End of the World?

- - -

Rip Van Winkle

God created this World.
For some time, He kept an eye on it,
and was happy to see that it was progressing well.
Then,
He closed his eyes for a moment,
just for one moment.

But,
one moment of God
is equivalent to
millennia of Human Beings.

When God opened His eyes,
just like Rip Van Winkle,
He found that,
the World created by Him
had changed totally,
and, it was difficult to recognise it.
The Son of Adam
had totally destroyed the Nature's balance.

continue..

God was dumbfounded.
He asked the Son of Adam –
"Can I not rely on you
for even one moment?"
The Son of Adam
Did not find it necessary to reply;
he was busy in his destructive activities.

God slapped his forehead with his palm.
He could do nothing other than
staring at the Son of Adam.

Actually,
No Rip Van Winkle-like sleeper
should wake up at all
even if he is God Himself.

- - -

Robinson Crusoe

One night
I saw a dream.

I was Robinson Crusoe,
Standing alone
on an island;
An island full of green plants
and diverse life-forms.
The ground
was full of hoards of animals,
The sky, full of flocks of birds,
The ocean, full of infinite fishes.

Suddenly,
A hurricane swirled.
It spread contamination in the air.
All greenery dried out,
All trees fell down.
All animals, birds, fishes
succumbed to injuries and epidemics,
and died.

continue..

The entire surrounding region
became barren.
Nothing else was left,
except the gloomy silence of Death.
Only I was left,
standing alone
amongst all the destruction.

And, I woke up suddenly,
Startled,
Sweating.
Oh! It was only a dream!
I wiped my sweat and got up.

And then,
I saw that,
A storm named Pollution
had swept in.
It was spreading poison everywhere.

. . . .

continue..

Drops of water
were filled up with Kalkoot poison.
Gusts of air
were full of Halaahal poison.
Poison was fouling every breath.
All greenery was drying up,
All trees were falling down.
All animals, birds, fishes,
were succumbing to injuries and epidemics,
and dying.
The surrounding region
was becoming barren.
Nothing else was going to be left,
except the gloomy silence of Death.
And there was I was,
Standing alone, amongst all the destruction,
The Robinson Crusoe of the new era!

*

continue..

What I did see,
with my eyes closed,
Was it a dream?
Or, was it reality?
What I am seeing now,
With my eyes open,
Is it a dream?
Or, is it real?
What is a dream, what is real?

I was mortally afraid,
And shut my eyes tight.
But that made no difference.
The storm named Pollution
whirled stronger and stronger.

- - -

Aladdin And The Jinn

Aladdin rubbed the Magic Lamp.
The Jinn appeared in front of him.
The Jinn saluted and asked –
'My Lord, I am at your service.
What service may I render?
Shall I bring sweets for you?
Or, perhaps a pleasant drink?
Shall I sing a melodious song?
Just say the word.
Your wish is my command.'

Aladdin ordered the Jinn –
'The Earth is full of pollution.
The environment is in danger.
Destroy the pollution forthwith.'

The petrified Jinn spluttered,
'I am ready to suffer any retribution,
But I urge you,
Do not order me to carry out this impossible task.
Several times in the past,
I have strived hard but failed miserably.
The humans generate pollution hundred times faster
Than my pace of its elimination.
The situation is just beyond salvation.

continue..

'But, My Lord,
there does exist a solution.
Either, the human beings mend their ways totally,
Or, the Human Race itself will have to be extinguished.

'My Lord,
The humans just won't stop their dastardly deeds.
Now, tell me,
Shall I terminate the Human Race?
Just say the word, My Lord.
Your wish is my command.'

Aladdin failed to utter a single word.

- - -

The Third Eye

Lord Brahma
is the creator;
He created this World.
Lord Vishnu,
in form of civilization,
nurtured the World, developed it.
Now it is the turn of
Lord Mahesh,
Shiva the Destroyer.
How and when will he arrive?

Now, the deeds of the human-race
will take the form of Lord Mahesh,
and will destroy the Earth
by opening the third eye
called Pollution.

- - -

Water Of Holy Ganges

In today's world,
is it right
to pour Ganges-water
in the mouth of a dying person?

Oh yes, definitely!
Even though
that water
is no more clean,
no more pure,
One thing is for sure –
On drinking it,
That person will surely die,
and, will begin his march towards Heaven.
Because, today
The Ganges-water
has turned poisonous;
it has taken the form of a Yamdoot
ready to take a person to the next world.
And, all this is
due to Pollution.

continue..

But, how does the Pollution matter?
All that anyone is concerned is –
Reaching Heaven.

So, my friend, don't wait;
Drink the Ganges-water,
whether pure or impure.

- - -

Bhasmasur

We are the modern Bhasmasur,
Destructive, intoxicated with power,
Determined to control the universe.
We constantly carry out dastardly deeds.
We are turning the Earth into ashes.

According to the Puranas,
The Lord has to come down to the Earth
in form of an incarnation,
for destroying villains.
The Lord himself visited the Earth
and annihilated Bhasmasur.

But this new Bhasmasur's end
will not be at the hands of the Lord.

Why so?

continue..
∽

It is believed that
One whose life ends at the hands of the Lord,
reaches Heaven,
howsoever wicked he may be.
But this modern Bhasmasur
is evil beyond imagination,
So much so that
by no chance does the Lord want him in Heaven.

Therefore,
Pollution the devil has been created
to bring about the end of this modern Bhasmasur.
And,
We are going to die by our own hand.
Because,
We ourselves have generated pollution
With our own hands!

- - -

Ramayan –
Yesterday's & Today's

Yesterday, the villains were
Khar and Dooshan;
Today's villain is Pollution.
Yesterday's challenge was
From Ravan, Lanka's emperor;
Today's challenge is
The imbalance in Nature.
Yesterday, Seeta was in danger.
Today, the glaciers,
due to rising temperature.
Yesterday, Laxman
got mortally injured;
Today, green forests
are getting slaughtered.
Yesterday, the mighty ocean
was causing an obstruction;
Today, the depleting water-level
is causing concern.
Yesterday, Hanuman,
the son of the Wind,
was Lord Ram's messenger;

continue..

Today, the poisonous wind
is the Death's harbinger.
Yesterday's enemy-generals were
Meghnad and Kumbhkarna;
Today's, every Human.
Yesterday, Lanka did burn;
Today, it is the Earth's turn.

Yesterday,
Seetamai was freed
from Ravan's clutches,
through Lord Ram's determination;
Today,
Mother Earth is to be freed
from Pollution's clutches,
Through common man's positive action.

- - -

Bakasur

The Human Being
is a Bakasur;
he is gobbling away
the Nature's treasures.

Another one,
a mighty being,
has now arrived
to stop this Bakasur the Human.
This mighty being is,
the Pollution.
Is this mighty one
a new Pandava,
a new Bheem?

Oh No!
This Pollution
has turned to be
another new Bakasur!!

Now, who will stop
this latest Bakasur,
this Pollution?

- - -

Shishupal

[Note: As per the Mahabharata, Lord Krishna, using his weapon Sudarshan Chakra, assassinated Shishupal, after Shishupal carried out 100 sinful deeds.]

The Homo Sapiens
Went on carrying out vile deeds,
On and On.
Father Time
Kept on forgiving him.
Then one day, Father Time told the Homo Sapiens,
"You have taken undue advantage of your position.
You have looted Mother Nature.
You have harmed the Earth.
You have put all living beings in danger.
Now the pot of your dastardly deeds is overflowing.
Enough is enough.
O Human,
O modern Shishupal,
Now, the 'Pradooshan Chakra',
The all-potent weapon called Pollution
Will bring your accursed existence to an end ".

- - -

Eklavya

Dronacharya was
an expert in the art of archery.
He was the inspiration
behind Eklavya's mastery,
though Dronacharya was unaware of this.
One day, he mat Eklavya.
Eklavya bowed and said,
"Whatever expertise I have achieved in archery,
is due to you, Sire".
On hearing this, Dronacharya said to Eklavya,
"Then give me your right thumb as an offering".
Eklavya replied, "What of the thumb, Sire,
I can offer even my life".
Aaying this, Eklavya cut off his thumb
And offered it to Dronacharya.

continue..

Today,
the Dronacharya of Kaliyug
is Manuputra, the son of Manu.
He is en expert in many arts.
He is the reason
behind neo-Eklavya's mastery,
though Manuputra is unaware of this.
Once Manuputra, the neo-Dronacahrya
Met the neo-Eklavya.
Neo-Eklavya said,
"Whatever I have achieved,
is due to you".
On hearing this, the neo-Dronacharya said,
"Then give your life as an offering".
Neo-Eklavya replied,
"What of giving my life,
I can even take your life".
And,
Before Manuputra, the neo-Dronacharya,
realized that
Kaliyug is different from Dwaparyug,
his chest was pierced
by the neo-Eklavya, named Pollution.

*

. . .

continue..

Is the Human Being
an expert, a master, like Dronachartya?
Is Pollution
like Eklavya?
Is Pollution becoming powerful
by drawing inspiration from the Human Being?

All this discussion is useless.
But, one thing is certainly true –
The poisonous arrow of Pollution
has pierced the heart of the Human Being.

- - -

Mahabharat Of Kaliyug

1. GANGA

This is a tale from
Mahabharat of Kaliyug.

She was Ganga,
River Ganges in human form.
She had agreed to become
King Shantanu's wife.
When the first child was born,
Ganga took it to the river,
dunked it,
and drowned it.
Shantanu watched helplessly from a distance,
but kept quite,
because, that's what Ganga's pre-condition was.

Such an event
took place the next time too,
and the next,
totally seven times.

continue..

When Ganga took the eighth infant
to the river, to drown it,
Shantanu stopped her.
Ganga handed over the new-born to Shantanu,
and told him,
"You don't understand that
for this infant, death is deliverance.
Seven were freed.
But now, this eighth child
will have to suffer
in this contaminated world,
and, it will have to die of pollution.
Don't you think that,
freeing it from this misery
was a much better option?
Any way,
Now it's too late.
Now keep this infant
and repent." . . .

Ganga disappeared.
Poor Shantanu
was left standing, dumbfounded,
holding the new-born child,
accompanied only by Pollution,
the harbinger of Death.

-

continue..

2. <u>YAKSHA</u>

This story
is from Mahabharat of Kaliyug.

Pandavas were in Van-vaas,
Living in the forest.
Once, Draupadi was thirsty.
One Pandava went to the nearby lake
to fetch water.
He saw a frightening entity.
He did not pay any attention to it,
filled up his pot.
Before turning back,
he took some water from the lake
in his cupped palms,
took a sip, and,
fell down, dead.

In the same way,
the second Pandava died.
Then the third,
And so also the fourth.

continue..

Finally,
Yudhishthira, the eldest and the wisest Pandava,
himself went to the lake.
He saw all four brothers lying dead,
and wondered what must have happened.
Just then, he saw a frightening entity.
'Possibly, it was the Yaksha,
the Guardian of the Lake',
so thought Yudhishthira.
He said to the entity,
"O Guardian of the Lake,
I am ready to answer all your questions.
Give my brothers their life back". . . .
The Entity replied,
"You call yourself learned;
Don't you know that,
I am not a Guardian,
I am a gobbler;
I am not a Yaksha,
I am Pollution.
Your brothers have drunk
Contaminated water;
they can never come back to life".

continue..

On hearing this,
Yudhishthira beat his head.
Answering all unasked questions,
He took a sip of the lake-water.

This time,
to reach Heaven,
Yudhishthira did not find it necessary
to climb the Himalaya;
Just a sip of polluted water
was enough,
just a sip.

-

3. **BHEESHMA**

This is
the Kurukshetra of Kaliyug.

A fierce battle was raging.
From hidden position,
Arjun emptied his gun on Bheeshma.
Bheeshma was injured grievously,
and fell down.
but he did not die,

continue..

Pandavas visited the injured Bheeshma.
Bheeshma requested Arjun,
"I am thirsty.
Give me some water to drink".
Arjun fetched water from a nearby tap.
As soon as the water touched Bheeshma's lips,
his life was extinguished.
He did not even wait for the arrival of Uttarayana.
. . . . .
The contaminated tap-water ensured that.

Did Arjun give
contaminated water unknowingly?
Or, did he know that
it was contaminated?
Or, did Bheeshma know in advance,
that it was contaminated?

No one will ever know.

-

4. **DURYODHAN**

This account is from
the end of the neo-Krukshetra war.

continue..

After losing the war,
Duryodhan hid underwater,
in a lake.
On getting to know this,
Pandavas reached the lake,
accompanied by Lord Krishna.

A discussion took place at the lake-shore.
Bheem said,
"Let us loudly denounce Duryodhan,
using foul language.
Our vile words will make him angry,
and he will come out.
I will then kill him in a wrestling duel".

Krishna said,
"I appreciate your confidence.
Yet, one can't predict for sure
the result of a duel.
Why take the trouble,
when there is a sure-shot way
to kill Duryodhan?

continue..

"Let him just stay underwater.
Hungry and thirsty,
how long will he stay there
with his nose pinched?

. . . . .

After some time,
he will be forced
to gulp some water.

The humans of Kaliyug
have contaminated all lakes.
Let Duryodhan drink the foul water,
and die on his own".

Thus,
Duryodhan's death
was ensured.

- - -

Elegy - 3

Cricket World-Cup

The final match
of Cricket World-Cup.

It was the Nature's turn to bat first.
It scored fours after fours,
it hit sixes:
Clean Environment,
plentiful water,
trees, green cover,
fruits, flowers, food grains.

Then it was the Human's turn to bat.
He started an aggressive inning,
and kept on hitting.
The first blow was on the Air's head;
the air got polluted.
The next stroke injured Water;
it got contaminated,
it started depleting.
Then one hit after another:
One blow struck trees and greenery,
One knocked out crops and food-grains,
One battered life-forms.
Everyone got a thumping, everyone was injured.

continue..
◦━

Finally,
The Human slugged out such a strong stroke,
that, the bat slipped out of his grip,
landed smack on the Nature
and whacked it heavily.
The Nature was badly injured.

Well, no matter.
The Human won the World-Cup.
He became the Champion
of the whole World.

But, the Human found that,
The Cup named Earth
had got heavily rusted;
it was breaking up, crumbling.

. . . . .

Now, what will the Human do
with a rusted, crumbling cup?

- - -

Life-Imprisonment

What crime have we committed
for which
we have been given
Life-imprisonment
in this 'Kaala Paani'?
Does no one care
that we are innocent?

Yes, there's water here;
But it is filthy,
and that too is getting depleted.
Yes, there's air;
But it is foul, contaminated.
Yes, there are life-forms around;
But they are being destroyed mercilessly.
Yes, there's land;
But it is turning barren.
Yes, there are ice-caps
on high mountain-peaks;
But they are melting one by one.
Yes, there are minerals under the ground;
But the stocks are getting exhausted.
Yes, there are Humans;
But they are bent upon performing Harakiri,
and, we are afraid,
that, tomorrow the whole Race may be dead.

continue..

Our forefathers loved the Nature.
But, the grown-ups of today
have lost their way.
Their ever-growing needs
are going beyond limits,
and the nature's balance
is being destroyed
by their ill-deeds.
We are just tiny tots and young children.
Yet, we have to suffer the consequences
of their irresponsible actions.

. . . .

Who will alleviate our misery?
When will that Messiah appear
who will transform this Hell
into a World Heavenly?
When?

- - -

Banished From Heaven

The Lord
created this Earth,
this heavenly Earth,
full of mineral-wealth;
He created fresh air & water,
He created tasty fruits
and flowers full of fragrance.
Then the Lord created
the Human Being.
After that
The Lord was tired,
and He took a short nap.

And,
the Human Being
became the Overlord
of this heavenly Earth,
its Emperor;
and started misbehaving.
He captured the whole Earth,
he started abusing and hurting
air, water, fruit, flowers, trees, creepers,
all life-forms.
All of them started withering,
started dying.

continue..

Just then,
The Lord opened His eyes.
Quoth He –
'O Human,
I gave you Heaven
But you are determined
To convert it into Hell.
So, now, suffer in this Hell.'

Lo and behold,
the Human's surroundings
transformed into
garbage, filth, gutters, pollution, disease.

. . . .

The Human started repenting.
But now it is too late.
Who will give salvation
to the Human
from this muck,
just who?

- - -

Incarnation

In my earlier incarnation,
I was the protector
of this Earth.
In the present life,
I am the gobbler
of this Earth.

In the earlier incarnation,
My feet touched the Earth
only after I bowed in front it.
In this life,
I am kicking the Earth repeatedly
and injuring it,
without any compunctions.

In the earlier incarnation,
I was teacher, a Guru;
I taught upliftment.
In this life,
I am Takshak Nag, the serpant,
ready to bite and kill the Earth.

continue..

In the earlier incarnation,
I was Hanuman,
who strived to locate Seetamai.
In this life,
I am neo-Ravana,
ready to locate means
to destroy Mother Earth.

In the earlier incarnation,
I was Laxman,
who could not protect Seeta
in the time of need,
despite his desire to do so.
In this life,
I am Duhshasan,
who is tearing up
the clothing of the Earth,
and have no desire to protect her.

. . . . .

If this goes on
in the same manner,
it is futile
to hope for the next incarnation;
it is indeed doubtful
whether I can complete
the present round of life itself.

- - -

We Believe

We believe, that
We are Lord Ram,
and that we, the Humans,
are conducting Ram-Rajya,
a just and fair reign,
on this Earth.
But, we are Ravan,
King of the Lanka called Pollution.

We believe, that
We are Lord Krishna,
showing the right direction
to confused Arjuns.
But, we are Duryodhan,
bent upon destroying
our own reign, this civilization.

We believe, that
we are Hanuman,
flying high
in this sky of progress.
But, we are Baali,
arrogant with own power.

continue..

We believe, that
we are God,
and that
the future of the entire universe
is in our own hands.
But, we are the Devil incarnate,
destroyers of the Nature,
annihilators of the Earth.

We believe, that
our Human race will continue
for ever and ever.
But, we are the new dinosaurs,
we will be extinguished all of a sudden,
due to this pollution.

. . . . .

When will we comprehend
the difference between
dreams and reality?
When?

- - -

One More Bhopal

A factory in Bhopal.
Number of activists clamouring,
warning that,
there could be a calamity anytime.
But nobody paid any attention.
And, one day,
Lots of poisonous gases leaked,
contaminating the atmosphere.
Thousands died,
Millions were afflicted.
Whole lot of households were ruined.
What an unimaginable tragedy!

Twenty five tears have passed,
but even now,
the affected populace
has not emerged from
the ill-effects of the poison.
And,
there is nobody to help them overcome.
How very sad!

continue..

How very sad!
Pollution is spreading fast
On this Earth.
Wise, knowledgeable persons
are clamouring,
warning that
anytime there could be
unimaginable calamities.
But nobody is paying attention.
And, one day,
The whole earth
will become contaminated like Bhopal.
How many will die?
How many will be afflicted?
How many households will be ruined?
Hundreds, thousands, millions?

. . . . .

And thereafter,
How long will the Human race
suffer the consequences?
How many decades?
Or, centuries?
Or, millennia?

continue..

Just think,
and calculate.
My mind has stopped functioning.
Perhaps,
the poisonous pollution,
the contamination,
has afflicted my brain.
Just like Bhopal.

- - -

Carbon-Credit

If the rich want to earn 'punya',
without making an effort,
there is a simple way –
Call priests
give them alms
give them tools to perform worship;
The priests will offer prayers,
they will chant Gods' eulogies,
and they will pass on the punya, the holy-credit,
to the rich host.
O affluent ones, be happy.
No need to strive yourselves;
Receive virtuous gains in exchange of money,
and extinguish your sins.

Just as
hoards of priests
carry out prayers and worship,
and just as their wealthy hosts
purchase the holy-credit from them;
Exactly in the same way,
poor nations
save fuel, save energy, save carbon-emission,
and collect purity-credit,
and, prosperous nations
purchase this purity-credit in exchange of money.

continue..

This is how
the two-way trade take s place –
One nation gets money,
the other nation takes charge of the credit.
This win-win swap is lauded as:
Carbon-Credit.

- - -

Elegy - 4

Some Sher

(NOTE: Sher are couplets. They are
a type of classical Persian & Urdu verse.)

Why do you complain about the flood?
The dam was so constructed by you,
　　　　　that its breaking up was inevitable.
*

Of course, the Human will go to Heaven.
After all, it too has to be transformed into Hell,
　　　　　just as he did to Earth.
*

You have awakened the slumbering pollution.
Now it has opened its third eye, like Shiva;
　　now you are bound to be charred completely.
*

The Homo Sapiens are not a carbon copy of Dinosaurs.
Yet, the end of both is supposed to be identical!
*

Can I call this a city?
It is in fact a garbage-dump.
*

continue..

I have given up hope that the Earth will become
        a paradise;
No choice but to strike a friendship with it,
                        even though it is pure hell!

*

Says the slum-shanty to the gutter –
'I don't like your company; see how clean I am!'

*

O Man, why did you harass Nature,
the young and beautiful lady?
Now you are getting a thorough whack
on your face!

*

O Man, you threw away flowers and chose thorns
No wonder you have Cactus in your hands.

*

The Lord banished Adam from Paradise to Earth
Now Adam's children have banished themselves
from Earth to Hell.

*

. . . . .

continue..

Bridges collapsed, buildings tumbled down,
roads ruptured
But, no earthquake is to be blamed, Humans are.

*

I get only half a bite to eat; and I am sad
That, tomorrow I won't get even that, because
pollution is eating up land's fertility.

*

All is not well with the age-old suicide program
Alas! pollution has dried up all wells!

- - -

Some Muktaks

(Muktak is a 4-lined Verse,
common in Sanskrit, Hindi, Marathi)

My heart wants a soft embrace
My heart is eager for touch of warm breath
But I do not desire the soft touch of a Vish-kanya
And I want to stay away from the touch of
venomous pollution.
*

Yes, of course, it is true
That, pollution is like a burning fire
But, we have no right to complain
Because, Human Beings are
the creators of this Pollution.
*

Somnath is full of grime,
Vrindaban is full of muck
Jagannathpuri has become
the abode of garbage
Dwarka is now filthy,
Haridwar is dirty
Kedarnath is melting, Ganges is unclean.
But, do not blame Pollution
for the contamination
O Human, it is you who has spread
this impurity-poison..

continue..

*

The venomous killer has struck
Foul smell of death is all-around
      On seeing destruction of Earth
         and the cadaver of civilization,
Pollution is proud of its achievement.

*

Heaven is perpetual happiness, Hell is full of agony
God is the ruler of Heaven, and
       the ruler of Hell is Satan
There's no doubt whether
      the Earth is Heaven or Hell
Here, there is agony of Pollution, and
     the ruler of Earth is the Human.

*

. . . . .

Rich folks are carefree
All restrictions are for the poor
Rich nations are enjoying consumption
Poor nations have to control emission.

*

Temples and mosques are empty
Towns and villages are desolate
The aggressor Pollution advances
The number of Humans reduces.

continue..

*

Ice melts in the glass,
increasing the pleasure of wine.
Ice melts in the glaciers
increasing the anxiety of the populace.

*

Whether a premier or a pauper
Whether rich or poor
Everybody's fate turned into ashes
When Pollution became the Emperor.

*

Everybody has to reach Yamlok
And render life's account to Chitragupta
What justification will you render
For giving rise to Pollution?

- - -

Rubais

(Rubai is a 4-lined Verse, common in Persian
& Urdu, and has travelled to other Indian languages)

Much damage the Humans have caused
                    in just years handful!
They have squandered everything that the Earth
        had donated since time immemorial
Humans! See the ramification of your action;
                  the Nature will now die!
Why have you snatched the Heaven from
future generations, and consigned them to Hell?
               *

The 'Environment Day' is celebrated
            only once a year
On that day, every one purports to be
                the Earth's protector
On all other days, all Humans try their best
To strike hundreds of mortal blows on the Nature!
               *

It's fun & games for the Human,
but the Earth is in tears
The union of Man & pollution
      has caused harm to the Nature
The human recites the words
"Nature's protection" solemnly

107

continue..

While thrusting his knife
               into the heart of his own future.
           *

Pollution does not take cognizance of
         a Priest or a Moulvi
It denies the difference
               between a temple and a mosque
It is far from Religion,
          and teaches the World equality
It gives every Human the same destiny:
           Swallowing poison from its flask.
           *

       . . . . .

Don't curse the Pollution;
             don't use foul language against it
Thank it, salute it, bow to it, O ignorant Human
Some time or the other, every one has to reach
               the world-beyond-life
The pollution is hastening your moment of
             ascent to the Heaven.
           *

Pollution does not differentiate
             between rich and poor
Humans of all strata die from its venom every day
Pollution benefits quacks all the more
They keep filling their pockets,
            but not one patient gets cured.
           *

continue..

The enemy is all-powerful;
                    fearing this foe is justified.
However strong our army may be,
                    our defeat is certain.
Swords, guns and cannons are impotent
                    against this adversary
Pollution is the undefeated Emperor of this World.

*

The fire that we started, has spread so much
Our house started burning,
                    but we didn't get to know
Now the blaze called Pollution
            is turning the civilization into ashes
Saving the Human Being is now totally useless.

*

Why have you forgotten God,
                    and started loving the Devil?
Have no doubt of the result:
            An assured place in Hell
You left Purity the divine entity, and
                    embraced the Vishkanya called Pollution
This hug is poisonous;
                    your end is now certain.

*

I have one regret in life, though thoroughly late
Only one thought plagues my mind day and night,
If only we had ended the Pollution's might
This slow death wouldn't have become our fate.

*

continue..

. . . . .

Call it a deluge or call it a monstrous tsunami
Which will sweep away this civilization
Or, you could call it a poison,
                    dissolving into our life bit by bit
Say what you like, but
                    just stay away from this Pollution.
                                        *

There's happiness in poverty, and asceticism is fun,
Life is full of tussle, while Death gives joy;
                    so say all saintly men.
I just couldn't get to poverty
                    nor ascend to asceticism
But, with Pollution's help,
                    I did reach the door-step of Death.
                                        *

The voyager in life has this complaint about fate –
'I was searching for a guide,
                    but found only a dacoit
For cleanliness, with great hope,
                    I looked at other Nations
Alas! it was they who had looted it,
                    to feed pollution'.

continue..

*

All places of worship are polluted,
            so also all meeting-places
Fruits and flowers are polluted all-round,
          so also the flower of human-life
Whatever be one's religion,
           there is no deliverance on death
All ashes are polluted,
           and so also are all skeletons.

- - -

More Rubais

We are in this wonderful tavern, the tavern of Life
We are the wine-drinkers; and the jug of desire
                                        is our friend
Death is the tavern-keeper, and is eyeing us
                                        eagerly
We are the Saqi, and we serve to ourselves
the poison of pollution.

*

It has stayed with us on this Road of Life
Even though we resisted, it kept pace all the time
It is ready to kill is, and is waiting to say 'fatiha'
The methods of Pollution are
                        beyond imagination indeed.

*

For a long time, I was hearing about
                                the impending arrival
It came and settled down, never to depart.
Now this house is its, more than mine.
This pollution will stay here till it sends me to my grave.

*

The race is like 'Formula One'; who will win?
Everyone ponders, but no one knows who will win
We are dazzled by our own speed, but,
The pollution still continues to be is ahead of us;
                                so who will win?

continue..

*

O my Beloved, I have found you;
now I am ready to face death
Because of you, I saw Heaven while still alive.
O Pollution, I you have found me;
                            now I desire only death
Because of you, Hell has eaten me alive.

*

No special assignment entrusted,
                        no instruction given
Neither is any pay given, nor a pat on the back
Still, this messenger of mine is working
                    day & night, without getting tired
Lord Yama says, 'This Pollution is doing
                            a great job'.

*

. . . . .

Homeopathy is of no use, allopathy is futile
No Vaid or Haqeem can cure this disorder
This malady is such that it has no cure
The disease called Pollution
                will kill the civilization, that's for sure.

*

:ontinue..

I am progressing; you have progressed
You dole out freely your advice on
                              Clean Environment
But, why did you not ponder on this at
                              Kyoto and Copenhagen -
'Who is spreading pollution,
                    and who has to bear its brunt?'
                              *

You may or may not be in your senses; I am
You may or may not have the requisite force; I have
It is a foregone conclusion,
            that I will send you on the path to Heaven
O Human, come into the embrace
                              of this Pollution.
                              *

The beloved resides in the eyes of the lover
Every breath of the lover is controlled by
                              his residential colony
The World controls the existence
                              of every colony
And, every pore of the world
                  is filled to the brim with pollution.
                              *

continue..

The Earth is distressed, and cries uncontrollably
The Nature is waiting, ready to sing 'marsiya'
Pollution has hit such a vicious blow, that
The civilization will die,
         and Time will build its mausoleum.
                   *

I believed that you would cause no harm
I didn't stop your vagabondish activities
O Pollution, I learnt the truth too late
I gave you my house, and you took my life!

- - -

Saqi: Wine-Server
Fatiha: Prayer for the dead.
Marsiya: A sad song of grief, Elegy

Haiku & Other Poems

(Note: Haiku is a type of classical Japanese verse. It is 3 lined.)

God created this world.
Then He created Man.
And, that was
       the beginning of the end of this world.
*

The seasons are changing.
Now Spring has no chance to follow winter.
Pollution has settled down, and refuses to depart.
*

The civilization is progressing.
Cholera and Plague have been eradicated, wiped out.
Now the populace will die from the epidemic called Pollution.
*

No Moon can be seen; but it this not Amavasya.
No Sun seen; but this is no Solar Eclipse.
Oh! the sky is perpetually overcast with Pollution!
[Amavasya: The no-moon night]
*

continue..

O Owl, do not utter thy unholy sound.
As it is, the whole world is dying due to Pollution.
No need for additional unholy omens now.
      [Note: In Indian tradition, the hooting of an owl
           is considered to be a bad omen.]
*

Now the Chaatak bird will remain thirsty
Now the peacock won't spread its dazzling fan
Because, it doesn't rain anymore; now
      acidic torrents pour down from the heavens.
*

This journey has been going on
      for thousands of years
Now it has reached the Final Destination;
Humans have created Pollution.
*

This is collective Hara-kiri.
Human race has thrust
Pollution-dagger in its own gut.
*

. . . . .

The whole world is a large cemetery.
Pollution is crushing us from all-around
It surges from air, land, sea-waves;
       and rams human droves into graves.

ntinue..

*

The edifice of civilization is towering high
But for how long?; the foundation is crumbling
Human society has given a NOC to Pollution.

(NOC- No Objection Certificate)
*

Dense fog, sharp descent, hidden path
The chariot of the son of man is hurtling down
    at breakneck speed
The terrain of pollution is murderous indeed!
*

Every day a new cemetery is added
Every day a new crematorium is created
The reign of pollution is boundless!
*

The train of civilization is full and fast
Terrorist Pollution causes a thundering blast
Scattering dead generations of tomorrow.
*

Heaven and Hell is an inseparable pair
Is that why humans push this Heaven named Earth
Into the embrace of the Hell called Pollution?
*

continue..
⊙⌒

'Is this the Earth or is this Hell?',
'What is the difference between the two?',
'There is less pollution in Hell.'

*

The 'Bullet-express' is about to stop.
This is not a station, it is the Terminus,
                    named Pollution, where
the train of civilization will stop permanently.

*

Rich men and rich countries
Are expert in increasing their wealth
And expert in increasing Pollution.

*

. . . . .

It is more damaging than bombs
More devastating than tsunami
It is the destructive Pollution-demon.

*

There's a shadow below each lamp.
Therefore the pedestal of dazzling civilization
Has been encircled by dark pollution.

*

continue..

The clock does not stop
The Pollution refuses to stop
What stops is, just
       the civilization's progress.
            *

'Happy New Year', said the Human Being.
'No Greetings for me', said the Earth,
'Greet Pollution; only **THAT** is happy'.
            *

Polluted dark fumes are emitted
By the flock of sparkling white cars
that follows the Environment-Minister.

- - -

Some More Haiku

Despite of a rampart, watch-towers, a moat,
The fort called the Nature is bound to fall.
Homo sapiens, the fort-keeper,
          is openly aiding Pollution, the enemy.

*

Excess load leads to load-shedding.
So, Nature is disconnecting for ever
The excess load called Human Race.

*

SERIAL KILLER
They are both serious killers.
Both are serial killers –
Man and Pollution.

- - -

Free Verse

1. It is said that –
   'There is hope till there is breath'.
   Today, our breath is stifled by pollution.
   Therefore,
   There is no hope of
   The continuance of civilization.

   *

2. One hunter
   One arrow
   One bird falls down dead.
   Sage Valmiki became a poet,
   And he composed Ramayana.

   Today the fowler named Pollution
   Is taking millions of lives.
   But –
   Even before his pen touches paper
   Today's Valimiki falls down dead.

   *

3. Man is the highest rung
   in Life's ascent.
   Pollution-rust is eating away the ladder
   Very soon, Homo Sapiens will become
   Another 'Neanderthal',
   Evolution's extinct link.

continue..

*

4. Be careful while riding this vehicle
    Heavy load, breakneck speed, no brakes
    The pollution- gradient is dangerous
    There is bound to be a grave accident.
    The civilization is bound to perish.

*

5. The human race is a fallen tree
    Flowing in the speedy river of Time
    Pollution is a mighty waterfall
    It will fling down this tree
    And shatters it into pieces infinite.

*

. . . . .

6. Now Eid can not be celebrated
    Nor the 'Karwa Chauth' festival
    Now the moon is hidden
    Due to pollution-fog.

*

7. O Chakor bird,
    Why chant the moon's name now?
    Why crave to see it?
    Chant the Earth's name instead;
    Because –
    Now the Earth too
    is fast becoming just like the moon:
    Beautiful from a distance
    but uninhabitable and baron.
    Oh yes,
    That's what pollution has done to the Earth!

continue..

*

8. The driver is the son of Adam.
   He napped at the wheel,
   And caused an accident
   to the car named civilization
   at the bend called pollution.

*

9. Yes, you may call me 'butshikan',
   the idol-destroyer.
   In the temple of my heart
   I had venerated the beautiful idol of Civilization.
   Today I have shattered that idol myself,
   After seeing the polluting acts of civilized humans.

*

10. Civilization is a chandelier
    Supported by a cord named Nature
    The lamp of civilization lights up the abode.
    The pollution-rat is nibbling at the cord
    The chandelier plummets
    And the Human race is crushed underneath.

*

11. The hutments hang their head with humiliation
    Skyscrapers have their nose in the air with pride.
    But why, when both are alike?
    Both generate pollution uniformly
    Both endanger environment equally.

*

. . . . .

continue..

12. Poor people try to save wealth.
    Poor Nations try to save fuel
    In the hope of wealth
    In the hope of Carbon-Credits.
                    *

13. I am relieved to see the Governmental Report,
    Because it says that
    'The pollution is reducing';
    Even though
    My stifled breath tells me otherwise.
                    *

14. The equations of environment
    are beyond comprehension.
    The level of ground-water is going down,
    Even though
    the speed of glacier-melting
    is increasing.
                    *

15. Enjoy the beauty of the Spring
    Enjoy the enchanting monsoon.
    All these will soon disappear
    More and more pollution will appear.
                    *

continue..

16. Do not look for an oasis in this arid desert
    Give up the hope of quenching your thirst.
    Now the whole world is a barren wasteland
    Now there's not a droplet of water in any oasis
    Now pollution has tightened its noose.
    Now –
    Thirst, only thirst
    Irrepressible thirst
    Now, one has to live a parched life
    And drink only bleeding tears.

- - -

Some More Free Verse

1. Homo Sapiens
    achieved first rank
    by copying the Devil.
    But, now he has been caught
    by God, the supervisor.
    And, now the Homo Sapiens
    has been rusticated from
    the exam named Life.
    *

2. Lot of behind-the-scene preparation
    is required
    before a news-item of a single sentence
    is published.

    Now, all preparation is complete.
    Only publication of the news-item remains,
    announcing the demise of
    Human Civilization.
    *

3. When a king is dying,
    someone else is ready
    to take his place.
    Who will be new king now?
    The present king of the World,
    the Homo Sapiens,
    is on the death-bed.

continue..

＊

4. A leader as seen on a dais
    is quite different from
    his face elsewhere.
    Now, the Homo Sapiens
    has become a big leader.
    He makes loud announcements
    of Saving the Nature,
    while
    he is murdering it himself.

＊

. . . . .

5. On the horizon,
    the fire-ball is swallowed by the ocean.
    The injured clouds are bathed in blood
    Bugle is being blown by every bird.
    A fierce battle rages
    Between Man and Pollution.

＊

6. Like insects, Humans live in cities
    Cities are strangled by python-like shanties.
    Every gutter, every road
    Every lane, every cross-road
    is full of muck.
    In every pipe, in every drain,
    plastic bags get stuck.
    Every metro, every suburb
    is in the grip of garbage.
    The serpent, pollution, has struck.

continue..

*

7. Save water.
    There is scant left
    Over land and underground.
    Save wood
    Save jungles, the green-cover.
    Save coal
    Save electric power
    Save air all-around.
    Rein in the contamination
    that is ever-increasing
    Curb the temperature
    that keeps rising and rising.
    Maintain the Nature's balance.
    Stop the Pollution's advance.
    Stop the destruction
    of civilization.
    Save the Human race
    from extinction.

- - -

Resurrection

Endangered

These innumerable endangered species,
Can they survive the strife
caused by this modern life?

New Mega-cities go on appearing
Jungles and mangroves are fast disappearing
The Human Juggernaut
razes wild habitats
with a powerful mace,
And then complains
with a straight face,
that, wild animals
are encroaching on his space!

At locale after locale,
groups of humans
are chanting slogans –
Save the Panda, Save the Whale
Save the Tiger, Save the Lion.
But to no avail.
No one listens.
And,
the endangered species are praying –
O God Almighty,
Save us
from the destructive Human Race.

continue..

O Humans,
Due to your deeds
species after species
will disappear,
One today; tomorrow, another
And on the day after tomorrow, yet another.
Yet you pay no heed,
You don't bother.
But what will happen one day
when it is the Human race's turn
to disappear?

. . . . .

O Humans,
Wake Up!
Don't you see
that,
Human Race too
Has become
An Endangered Specie!

continue..

Who but you yourselves
Can save
This Endangered Human Race,
O Humans?
Yes, That's a fact!
So,
Don't wait,
Don't hesitate,
Get up and ACT!
Act Now!
JUST NOW!

- - -

We All Are Arjuns

All of us
Are Arjuns.   1

In every person's mind,
At some critical moment,
There arises a conflict –
What should I do,
What should I not do?
Which path should I choose?
Questions, more questions.
Difficult questions, important questions,
Questions of life and death.   2

Even today,
All of us
Are standing
At the doorstep of
Mahabharata War.
In fact,
Not one, but several wars
Are knocking at our door –

continue..

War against poverty,
War against slums,
War against corruption,
War against the ever-rising-cost-of-living,
And, hundreds of other wars.
O yes,
And if we can get some free time,
Then,
We also have to fight a war
Against Pollution.
The true life-and-death war
Is in fact that one.   3

But we don't have Lord Krishna
With us;
And, there is no chance of
Getting his guidance.

                      . . . . .

Yes,
Without him,
All of us humans
Are Arjuns,
Totally confused Arjuns,
Empty-handed Arjuns,
Having relinquished our bows. 4

continue..

The War against Pollution
Is not even started
By us confused Arjuns,
Nor will it ever start.
The question of winning it
Just does not arise.

UNLESS .....
Unless we Arjuns
Ourselves become
KRISHNA.   5

- - -